THE LITTLE BOOK OF GREAT WOMEN

First published in the UK by
New Internationalist Publications Ltd
55 Rectory Road
Oxford
OX4 1BW, UK

www.newint.org

The Little Book of Great Women

Compilation © New Internationalist 2000; revised edition 2009;
reprinted 2010.

Printed on recycled paper by C&C Offset Printing Co. Ltd., China.

Designed by Peter Mays at white space.

British Library Cataloguing-in-Publication Data.

A catalogue record for this book is available from the British Library.

ISBN 978-1-906523-22-0

HE LITTLE BOOK OF

GREAT

WOMEN

New Internationalist

Foreword

'For most of history, Anonymous was a woman,' wrote Virginia Woolf.

Well, that's as may be, but thankfully many women have put their name to their utterances – be they wise or wild, sedate or seditious, holy or hilarious.

This little book is packed with a scintillating mix from women around the world. Dip in and you'll find eco-feminist Vandana Shiva rubbing shoulders with queen-of-outrage Mae West.

But one word of warning before you turn these pages: forget *Little Women*. Forget demure damsels, neatly tucked into the mental corsets of patriarchy. This book contains material from women who changed the world – or at least had the guts to try.

Half the sky

We have to free half of the human race, the women, so that they can help to free the other half.

Emmeline Pankhurst (1858-1928)
British suffragette.

High price

Women pay dearly with their freedom and dignity to obey the laws of marriage and the patriarchal class system that dominates society. Women also pay dearly in order to become free and escape domination.

Nawal el Saadawi (1931-) Egyptian writer.

Face value

I grew up with the need to prove that a 'half-caste', a 'nigger' and 'orphan child' could be a whole person. It took a long time for me to discover that I had a value.

May Optiz (1981-) Afro-German writer.

Now you see it, now you don't

To live in a culture [TV, adverts] in which women are routinely naked where men aren't is to learn inequality in little ways all day long.

Naomi Wolf (1962-) US writer.

Sexual revolution

Norman Mailer remarked during the 1960s that the problem with the sexual revolution was that it had gotten into the hands of the wrong people. He was right. It was in the hands of men.

Andrea Dworkin (1946-2005) US writer.

Fruits of development

Reproductive health, sexual health, family planning, and autonomy and equality for women are not the fruits of development; they are not even fertilizer - they are the tree itself.

Dr Nafis Sadik (1938-) head of the United Nations Population Fund (UNFPA).

Equity

The truth is, in order to get things like universal health care and a revamped education system, then someone is going to have to give up a piece of their pie so that someone else can have more.

Michelle Obama (b 1964) US attorney.

One for all

Either all human beings have equal
rights, or none have any.

Annie Besant (1847-1933)
British social reformer, speaking on India.

Women's love

You can't find home cooking in a can
Or clean air in a traffic jam.
You can't find a woman's love in a man
Never in a million years.

Alix Dobkin, contemporary US singer.

Being oneself

If I am opinionated and independent, if I am stuck in my ways, if I am a little off centre, so what? That is me.

Dr Elisabeth Kübler-Ross (1927-2004)
Swiss-born US psychiatrist and writer.

Warped minds

The image of a rapist appeals to some men, who identify it with being strong and virile, passionate and powerful.

Shere Hite, contemporary US sociologist.

Indomitable

A mid suffering, ruin and death, I had above all known love and the indestructible human capacity to survive and to pursue happiness.

Jung Chang (1952-   ) Chinese writer.

Who's to blame?

I am not bush, lion, savagery
mine are the sinews which built your cities
my sons fighting your wars
gave you victory, prestige
wherein lies the savagery in Africa.

Grace Akello (b1940s) Ugandan poet.

Religious oppression

To rule by fettering the mind through fear of punishment in another world is just as base as to use force.

Hypatia (c370-415) Egyptian philosopher and mathematician.

Colour of race

Whites ask another white - 'Why do you talk to her? She's not white!'
Blacks hiss at blacks, 'leave that honkey alone!'
I am that one.
The one in question.

Red Jordan Arobateau (b1943) Honduran/US writer.

Dreaming dreams

To seek visions, to dream dreams, is essential and it is also essential to try new ways of living, to make room for serious experimentation, to respect the effort even when it fails.

Adrienne Rich (1929-   ) US poet.

Misogyny

W omen have very little idea of how much men hate them.

Germaine Greer (1939-   )
Australian academic and writer.

Colour of earth

I think the kind of landscape that you grew up in, it lives in you. I don't think it's true of people who've grown up in cities so much, you may love a building but I don't think you can love it in the way that you love a tree or a river or the colour of the earth.

Arundhati Roy (1961-   )
Indian writer and activist.

Power of peace

Remember, each one of us has the power to change the world. Just start thinking peace, and the message will spread quicker than you think.

Yoko Ono (b 1933) artist and musician.

Schooldays

In school I learned to read, to write, and to get along. But I can't say that school really helped me to understand life. I think that education in Bolivia [despite reforms] is still part of the capitalist system we live in.

Domitila Barrios de Chungara
(1937-   ) Bolivian activist.

Ride the wind

I only want to ride the wind and walk the waves, slay the big whale of the Eastern sea, clean up the frontiers and save the people from drowning. Why should I imitate others, bow my head, stoop over and be a slave? Why resign myself to menial housework?

Trieu Thi Trinh (c245AD)
Vietnamese peasant woman leader.

On being proactive

Presenting women as 'victims' goes hand-in-hand with discrimination. We must become the protagonists in our own struggle.

Elena, member of a weaving collective from Guatemala, exiled in Mexico.

Trees

Trees are soul people to me, maybe not to other people, but I have watched the trees when they pray, and I've watched them shout and sometimes they give thanks slowly and quietly.

Bessie Harvey (1928-1995) US sculptor.

Natural reason

*W*e [women] are educated to the grossest ignorance and no art omitted to stifle our natural reason.

Mary Wortley Montague (1689-1762)
British writer and scientist.

Pornography

Until the mid-1960s, pornography was a male experience. But in the 1970s 'beauty pornography' crossed over into the female cultural arena, in women's magazines' adverts - like the one for Obsession perfume where a well-muscled man drapes the naked, lifeless body of a woman over his shoulder.

Naomi Wolf (1962-) US writer.

Born a slave

I was born a slave; but I never knew it till six years of happy childhood had passed away... I never dreamed I was a piece of merchandise.

Harriet Jacobs (c1813-1897)
US writer and former slave.

Party time

R evolution is the festival of the
oppressed.

Germaine Greer (1939-   )
Australian academic and writer.

Interconnectedness

We need policies of eco-justice, and we need to realize the spiritual dimensions of our life, of our interconnected planet Earth, of each other!

Petra Kelly (1947-1992)
German Green politician.

Seen and not heard

I am reminded that a great compliment of my childhood was 'She's such a quiet girl'.

Michelle Cliff (1946-) Jamaican writer.

Revenge

Interpretation is the revenge of the intellect upon art.

Susan Sontag (1933-2004) US critic.

Drinking it in

Prohibition came through a combination of business men who wanted to get more out of their workers, together with a lot of preachers and a group of damn cats who threw fits when they saw a workingman buy a bottle of beer but saw no reason to bristle when they and their women and little children suffered under the curse of low wages and crushing hours of toil.

Mary Harris Jones 'Mother Jones' (1837-1930)
US trade union activist.

God's pattern

I happen to think that a belief in God is all that is necessary for the acceptance of death, since you know that death, like life, is part of God's pattern.

Eleanor Roosevelt (1884-1962)
US politician and diplomat.

Long journey

I am woman, watch me grow
See me standing toe to toe,
As I spread my loving arms across the
land,
But I'm still an embryo,
With a long, long, way to go
Until I make my brother understand...
I am woman.

Helen Reddy (1941-   ) US singer.

Art

True art always comes from a cultural necessity.

Elizabeth Catlett (1919-   ) US artist.

Tenacity

I've got a woman's ability to stick to a job and get on with it when everyone else walks off and leaves it.

Margaret Thatcher (1925-   ) British politician.

Life without end

I am incapable of accepting infinity, and yet I do not accept finity. I want this adventure that is the context of my life to go on without end.

Simone de Beauvoir (1908-1986)
French philosopher and writer.

Space age

T he thing that I have done throughout my life is to do the best job that I can to be me.

Mae C Jemison (1957-   ) US astronaut.

Small is powerful

The *charkha* (spinning wheel) became an important symbol of freedom not because it was big and powerful, but because it was small; it could come alive as a sign of resistance and creativity in the smallest of huts and poorest of families. In smallness lay its power.

Vandana Shiva, contemporary Indian physicist and ecologist.

Angel child

I ain't good looking but I'm somebody's angel child.

Bessie Smith (1894-1937) US singer.

Hang on to the future

When you realise the value of all life, you dwell less on what is past and concentrate more on the preservation of the future.

Dian Fossey (1932-1985) US primatologist.

Feet and necks

I ask no favours for my sex. All I ask is that [men] take their feet from off our necks.

Sarah Grimké (1792-1873)
US abolitionist and feminist.

Ideas and loneliness

Life is difficult: a glory and a punishment. Ideas are excitement, glamorous company. Loneliness eats into me.

Vivian Gornick (1935-)
US journalist and academic.

Extraordinary people

I don't believe in ordinary or extraordinary people, unless we are all extraordinary.

Carol Shields (1935-2003) US/Canadian writer.

You hold the power

'Cause a rose is still a rose
Baby, girl, you're still a flower
He can't lead you and then take you
Make you and then break you
Baby, girl, you hold the power.

Aretha Franklin (1942-   ) US singer.

Winning

Whoever said 'It's not whether you win or lose that counts' probably lost.

Martina Navratilova (1956-   )
Czech/US tennis player.

Aspiration

Attempt the impossible in
order to improve your
work.

Bette Davis (1908-1989) US film actress.

Growing older

Life begins later than you think.
Carol Shields (1935-2003) US/Canadian writer.

Tolerable world

When you make a world tolerable for yourself, you make a world tolerable for others.

Anaïs Nin (1903-1977) US writer.

Life or death

Razors pain you;
Rivers are damp;
Acids stain you;
And drugs cause cramp.
Guns aren't lawful;
Nooses give;
Gas smells awful;
You might as well live.

Dorothy Parker (1893-1967) US writer and critic.

Escape

If I was a man I would not let my children live in this miserable hole [the favela/slum]. If God helps me to get out of here, I'll never look behind me.

Carolina Maria de Jesus (1915-1977)
Brazilian woman, in the 1950s.

Imbalance

As with most liberal sexual ideas, what makes the world a better place for men invariably makes it a duller and more dangerous place for women.

Julie Burchill (b 1959), UK journalist.

Survival

We have a special responsibility to the ecosystem of this planet. In making sure that other species survive we will be ensuring the survival of our own.

Wangari Maathai, contemporary
Kenyan environmentalist.

The child inside

Another belief of mine: that everyone else my age is an adult, whereas I am merely in disguise.

Margaret Atwood (1939-   ) Canadian writer.

Where we live

The environment is where we all live; and development is what we all do in attempting to improve our lot within that abode. The two are inseparable.

Gro Harlem Brundtland (1939-) when Prime Minister of Norway, addressing the UN in 1988.

Social injustice

f the market is left to sort matters out,
social injustice will be heightened and
suffering in the community will grow with
the neglect the market fosters.

Helen Clark (b 1950) former Prime Minister of
New Zealand.

Warriors of the Sea

Everybody knows that the whale is smarter than we

Probably that's why we call him the king of the sea

We're killing everything on dry land, why don't we just let the fishes be

Some of us are Greenpeace Warriors of the Sea.

Joan Baez (1941-   )
US singer/songwriter, in 1982.

Enthusiasm

You will do foolish things, but do them with enthusiasm.

Colette (1873-1954) French writer.

Do it

I don't know everything, I just do everything.

Toni Morrison (1931-   ) US writer.

Fiery love

Love is a fire. But whether it is going to warm your hearth or burn down your house you can never tell.

Joan Crawford (1906-1977) US actress.

Good for nothing?

Hungry people cannot be good at learning or producing anything, except perhaps violence.

Pearl Bailey (1918-1990) US singer.

Let go

Nothing is permanent. You don't want to possess anything that is dear to you because you might lose it.

Yoko Ono (1933-)
Japanese/US musician and artist.

Women love

In loving another woman I discovered the deep urge to both be a mother to and find a mother in my lover... I treasure and trust the drama between two loving women.

Sue Silvermarie, contemporary US poet.

Forest home

This forest is our mother's home
We will protect it with all our might.

Women of Reni village in India.

Savaged by TV

I'm always amazed that people will
actually choose to sit in front of the TV
and just be savaged by stuff that belittles
their intelligence.

Alice Walker (1944–   ) US writer.

Useful man

I've got water, electricity, my children have enough to eat [but] I miss a man. A man has more prestige than a woman. He inspires more respect. It is useful to have one at your side.

Fatma, an Egpytian woman whose husband lives with his other wife.

My home

Home is within me. I carry everyone and everything I am with me wherever I go.

Suheir Hammad (1973-   ) Palestinian/US poet.

Hell

From time immemorial
Hell was invented
to frighten the poor
with its eternal punishments.

Violeta Para (1904-1967) Chilean poet.

The scaffold and the struggle

I f they want to hang me, let them. And on the scaffold I will shout 'Freedom for the working class!'

Mary Harris Jones 'Mother Jones'
(1837-1930) US trade union activist.

Fancy footwork

Part of the joy of dancing is conversation. Trouble is, some men can't talk and dance at the same time.

Ginger Rogers (1911-1995) US entertainer.

Pasta pasta

Everything you see I owe to spaghetti.

Sophia Loren (1934-   ) Italian actress.

Risk-taking

Risk! Risk anything! Care no more for the opinions of others... Act for yourself. Face the truth.

Katherine Mansfield (1888-1923) New Zealand/British writer.

Borne in mind

Feminists have studied and thought, and they want to make changes that will benefit all of society. Throughout the world, some women are still being sold, beaten, raped and killed, so this is a struggle that must be in the minds of all women.

Simone de Beauvoir (1908-1986)
French philosopher and writer.

Sharing husbands

A shared husband I don't want!
I want my own.

Chichewa song, Malawi.

Eternal youth

The secret of staying younger is to live honestly, eat slowly, and lie about your age.

Lucille Ball (1911-1989) US entertainer.

Applaud each victory

Even the smallest victory is never to be taken for granted. Each victory must be applauded, because it is so easy not to battle at all, to just accept and call that acceptance inevitable.

Audre Lorde (1934-1992) US writer and poet.

Brighter dawn

The history of human growth and development is at the same time the history of the terrible struggle of every new idea heralding the approach of a brighter dawn.

Emma Goldman (1869-1940) US revolutionary and writer.

Honesty

Oh, I'm so inadequate – and I love myself!

Meg Ryan (1962-) US actress.

Daring

When I dare to be powerful, to use my strength in the service of my vision, then it becomes less and less important whether I am afraid.

Audre Lorde (1934-1992) US writer and activist.

Noble aim

My object was to die, and if to die, to die nobly fighting against this despotic system of Government, which had kept my country in perpetual subjection.

Bina Bhowmick after shooting at Sir Stanley Jackson, Governor of Bengal, in 1932.

Touch the books

Dance! Rejoice!
   Those who said
it is evil for women to touch books
are dead....

Subramanya Bharati, Tamil poet, in 1920.

Life lessons

What matters most is that we learn from living.

Doris Lessing (1919-   ) British novelist.

Drops of learning

Gather what little drops of learning you can, and consider them a great treasure.

Christine de Pisan (c1363-1430) Italian scholar.

New African

Don't worry to define my race. I've defined myself thoroughly in my novels. I am a New African. I like being a pioneer, creating light and space.

Bessie Head (1937-1986)
South African/Botswanan writer.

Scary

All the men [in a group] were able to face the fact that they were really quite scared of women and that deep down women's equality, and separateness especially, made them uneasy.

Susie Orbach and **Luise Eichenbaum**,
British psychotherapists.

Education - the key

Educate your women and the nation will take care of itself.

Sarojini Naidu (1879-1926) Indian social reformer.

Dedicated to....?

If you start to write a poem
think first of who will read it.

Clementina Suárez (1902-1991) Honduran poet.

Cultural identity

We will demonstrate that we are flourishing cultures, and are changing the 'cultural pollution' we are submitted to and the image of backwardness and poverty that has been thrust upon us.

Rigoberta Menchu (1959-   )
Guatemalan indian activist.

Visible vision

Realism is simply the tool I use to make my vision visible.

Christine Pflug (1936-1972) German artist.

Motherland

The motherland for me is in every corner, it's also in the miners, in the peasants, in the people's poverty, their nakedness, their malnutrition, in their pains and their joys.

Domitila Barrios de Chungara (1937-)
Bolivian activist, speaking in 1975.

Skin colour

We were Black Americans in West Africa, where for the first time in our lives the colour of our skin was accepted as correct and normal.

Maya Angelou (1928-   ) US writer.

Paint it black

After I decided to become an artist, the first thing that I had to believe was that I, a black woman, could penetrate the art scene and that I could do so without sacrificing one iota of my Blackness, or my femaleness, or my humanity.

Faith Ringgold (1930-   ) US artist.

Knowledge

Age is getting to know all the ways the world turns, so that if you cannot turn the world the way you want, you can at least get out of the way so you won't get run over.

Miriam Makeba (1932-2008) South African singer and civil rights activist.

Writing rainbows

I feel this is the pot-luck of a writer's life. One day there is absolutely nothing and the next day there is a big rainbow.

Bessie Head (1937-1986)
South African/Botswanan writer.

Go for it

Let's be shameless. Be greedy. Pursue pleasure. Avoid pain. Wear and touch and eat and drink what we feel like. Tolerate other women's choices. Seek out the sex we want and fight fiercely against the sex we do not want. Choose our own causes. And once we break through and change the rules so our sense of our own beauty cannot be shaken, sing it and dress it up and flaunt it and revel in it: in a sensual politics, female is beautiful.

Naomi Wolf (1962-) US writer.

Democracy

Nudge Burma to democracy.
Aung San Suu Kyi (1945-   ) leader of the
National League for Democracy in Burma.

Herstory

The key to understanding women's
history is in accepting - painful
though it may be - that it is the history of
the majority of the human race.

Gerda Lerner (1920-   ) US historian.

Seeking the sisterhood

Feminists can't seem to figure out why their movement isn't growing. Could the fact that feminism uses universities as its major site of recruitment, rather than jails, halfway houses, day care centres, churches, restaurants, the streets, mommy blog communities… have something to do with it?

Brownfemipower, contemporary blogger and writer.

Shaping destiny

To reclaim our past and insist that it become a part of human history is the task that lies before us, for the future requires that women, as well as men, shape the world's destiny.

Judy Chicago (1939-) US artist.

Reading the signs

Men and women make sad mistakes about their own symptoms, taking their vague uneasy longings, sometimes for genius, sometimes for religion, and oftener still for a mighty love.

George Eliot (1819-1880) British writer.

Taking leave

Most beautiful of things I leave is sunlight;
then come glazing stars and the moon's face;
then ripe cucumbers and apples and pears.

Praxilla (c450BC- ?) Greek poet.

Brevity

Brevity is the soul of lingerie.
Dorothy Parker (1893-1967) US writer and critic.

Ways of thinking

There are ways of thinking that we don't know about. Nothing could be more important or precious than that knowledge, however unborn. The sense of urgency, the spiritual restlessness it engenders, cannot be appeased.

Susan Sontag (1933-2004) US writer and critic.

Ownership

The Desert has its own moon
Which I have seen
With my own eye
There is no flag on it.

Alice Walker (1944-) US poet and writer.

Private is political

It is necessary to undo the separation between the private and the public because in this separation lies the oppression of women and the poor.

Nawal el Saadawi (1931-) Egyptian writer.

Comfortable things

I am always looking for comfort in a world disturbingly subject to change. Sometimes I find it in objects, things that sit still for a while and slowly gather, then release their energy.

Liz Magor (1948-) Canadian artist.

Hostile nature

Alone in the woods I felt
The bitter hostility of the sky and the trees
Nature has taught her creatures to hate
Man that fusses and fumes.

Stevie Smith (1902-1971) British poet.

Determination

I am going to keep on drawing until they tell me to stop. If no one tells me to stop, I shall make them even after I am dead.

Pitseolak (1904-1983) Canadian Inuit artist.

Force full

I was sure that no force, not even machine guns, could stop the raid.

Kamaladevi Chattophadhyaya (1903-1990)
Indian activist, speaking of the 1930 raid on
salt fields near Bombay that she organized.

The scream

A good many dramatic situations begin with screaming.

Jane Fonda (1937-   ) US actress.

What you can do

It doesn't matter where a human being lives, as long as their contribution to life is constructive, not destructive.

Bessie Head (1937-1986)
South African/Botswanan writer.

Snakes and slaves

Hot weather brings out snakes and slaveholders, and I like one class of the venomous creatures as little as I do the other.

Harriet Jacobs (c1813-1897)
US writer and former slave.

Indonesia

I am a good citizen. I never overspeed on the road. I never steal, I always cross the street in the right place. But I'm definitely against the Government!

Dita Sari, contemporary, Indonesian democracy activist jailed by Suharto.

Saying No

You know, that woman speaks 18 languages, and she can't say 'no' in any of them.

Dorothy Parker (1893-1967) US writer and critic.

Stand on your own feet

Because I work I feel more free than other women. I am able to solve my own economic problems. I can educate my children. I don't depend on anybody for anything.

Factory worker in Mozambique.

Size matters

Perhaps that's what the 21st century has in store for us. The dismantling of the Big. Perhaps it will be the Century of Small Things.

Arundhati Roy (1961-)
Indian writer and activist.

Free speech

Many creative women and men in Africa have decided to fight back against oppression in defence of the right to express their ideas and thoughts with freedom.

Nawal el Saadawi (1931-   ) Egyptian writer.

Plant the seed

A narchists or revolutionists can no more be made than musicians. All that can be done is to plant the seeds of thought.

Emma Goldman (1869-1940)
US revolutionary and writer.

Inspired leadership

We should ask all our leaders: 'Are you doers? Will you solve our problems, and not hide or deny them? Will you reject the politics of division and retribution and inspire people to come together?' Because real leadership is about healing racial divides, not exploiting them for personal or political reasons.

Hillary Rodham Clinton (1947-   )
US lawyer and politician.

Those were the days

Childhood is laughter too. Playing in the sand or rollerskating, learning how to ride a bicycle. Laddering a thousand pairs of tights and accepting Mother's anger as the price of a wonderful day.

May Optiz (1981-   ) Afro-German writer.

Expectations

All the average human being asks is something they can call home; a family that is fed and warm; now and then a little happiness; and once in a long while an extravagance.

Mary Harris Jones 'Mother Jones' (1837-1930) US trade union activist.

Perspectives

From a world in which life or death, victory or defeat, national survival or national extinction had been the sole issues, I returned to a society where no one discussed anything but the price of butter.

Vera Brittain (1893-1970) British writer, at the end of World War I.

Power of eloquence

It seemed to me then, and for many years after, that the spoken word hurled forth among the masses with such wonderful eloquence, such enthusiasm and fire, could never be erased from the human mind and soul.

Emma Goldman (1869-1940)
US revolutionary and writer.

Child teachers

I have learnt precious lessons from all my children.

Angelica Garnett (1918-) British artist.

Everyday things

The extent to which we take everyday objects for granted is the precise extent to which they govern and inform our lives.

Margaret Visser, contemporary Canadian writer.

Food fact

The sad fact is that the stomachs of rich and poor alike very often have more fuel, and more of the wrong fuel, pumped into them than they need or can contend with.

Reay Tannahill (1929-2007) Scottish writer.

Essence of Africa

The geographical position [the Ngong hills in Kenya], and the height of the land combined to create a landscape that had not its like in all the world. There was no fat on it and no luxuriance; it was Africa distilled up through six thousand feet, like the strong and refined essence of a continent.

Isak Dinesen/Karen Blixen
(1885-1962) Danish writer.

Shells shock

I can't express what it means to hear the guns for the first time! It is a sensation so vast and lonely and crowded and cosmic all at once that one seems born into a new phase of existence where the old ways of feeling things do not answer any longer.

'Mademoiselle Miss', an American nurse in a French army hospital during World War I.

Barred thought

Imprisonment in my country is always a possibility for any person who thinks and writes freely.

Nawal el Saadawi (1931-) Egyptian writer.

Precarious paradise

I now see my childhood as a precarious paradise, slung like a cradle over a cloud, but none the less full of delight.

Angelica Garnett (1918-   ) British artist.

English rules

Sometimes I think of the English language as a pale skin that has covered up my flesh, the broken parts of my world.

Meena Alexander (1951-   )
Indian-American poet and author.

Imprisonment

For the first fifty-six days of my detention in solitary... a black iron bedstead became my world... my retreat.

Ruth First (1925-1982) South African journalist and anti-apartheid activist.

Mr Booze

My relationship with my husband has been difficult because he drinks. When a man drinks too much he loses his sense of morality.

Claudia, kitchen assistant in shantytown near Guatemala City.

Essentials

Three be the things I shall have till I die:
Laughter and hope and a sock in the eye.

Dorothy Parker (1893-1967) US writer and critic.

No entry

Were Jesus Christ himself to visit South Africa, he would be treated as a 'prohibited immigrant'.

Vijaya Lakshmi Pandit (1900-1990)
Indian nationalist and diplomat, in a 1946 UN debate
with South Africa's Field Marshall Smuts.

The great dictator

Passion will be not be commanded. It commands us.

Jeanette Winterson (1959-   ) British writer.

Non-violence

Non-violent opposition has led to results in a large number of countries. It will also be the case here.

Aung San Suu Kyi (1945-) leader of the National League for Democracy in Burma.

Lucky and unlucky

I think everybody is equal. The difference is that those who have an education are lucky and they should have more of a conscience. But they don't, they crush you if they can.

Dona Irma, street-market trader, Guatemala, in 1988.

Housebound

A house does not need a wife any more than it does a husband.

Charlotte Perkins Gilman (1860-1935) US writer.

Paying for health

There are very good things about Western medicine. [But] traditional medicine is more about sharing and helping one another, and if you are paid it's related to how much the patient can afford.

Yolanda, health promoter, Guatemala.

Circle of life

As Indian people, we believe we are all part of the sacred circle of life that has no beginning or end. There is a sacred energy that connects us in this circle. As you come back to the circle, know there is space waiting for you.

Sandra White Hawk (b 1953) of the First Nations Orphan Association in the US.

View from below

Women don't have the same freedom as men. The same rights, maybe. But we are looked down upon. Our dignity is taken away from us.

Claudia, kitchen assistant in
shantytown near Guatemala City.

Where there's a will

One day seven years ago I found myself saying to myself, I can't live where I want to, I can't go where I want to go, I can't do what I want to - I can't even say what I want to. I decided I was a very stupid fool not to at least paint as I wanted to.

Georgia O'Keeffe (1887-1986)
US artist, speaking in 1923.

Needing space

Fond as we are of our loved ones, there comes at times during their absence an unexplained peace.

Anna Shaw (1847-1919) US suffragist.

Counting

Two is a good number.

Carol Shields (1935-2003) US/Canadian writer.

More, more!

Too much of a good thing can be wonderful.

Mae West (1892-1980) US actress.

Learning to cope

*W*alk away from it until you're stronger. All your problems will be there when you get back, but you'll be better able to cope.

Lady Bird Johnson (1912-2007)
US writer and former 'first lady'.

Playing the game

I always wanted to be somebody. If I made it, it's half because I was game enough to take a lot of punishment along the way, and half because there were a lot of people who cared enough to help me.

Althea Gibson Darben (1927-2003) US tennis player.

Inner strength

My family directly and my people indirectly have given me the kind of strength that enables me to go anywhere.

Maya Angelou (1928-   ) US writer.

Jobs for the boys

The only jobs for which no man is qualified are human incubator and wet nurse. Likewise, the only job for which no woman is or can be qualified for is a sperm donor.

Wilma Scott Heide (1921-1985)
US nurse and feminist.

Thoughts and words

I have found thoughts and words to be the foundation for success and failure in life. I'm teaching my kids when to whisper and when to shout.

Diana Ross (1944-   ) US singer.

Link arms

Sisters, sing for all you're worth,
Arms are made for linking,
Sisters, we're asking for the earth.

> **Greenham Common Women's Peace Camp** song.
> Greenham Common in Berkshire, UK, was where US
> Cruise Missiles were based in the 1980s.

Stuck in the mud

Men are more conventional than women and much slower to change their ideas.

Kathleen Norris, contemporary US poet.

What's inside

Every woman more or less carries feminism inside herself - this is her woman's nature. My mother will never say she is a feminist but I have learned from her much of what I recognize as being feminist theory and practice.

Duska Andrie-Ruzicic, of the Psychotherapy Centre for women in Bosnia-Herzogovina.

Fair play

Men, their rights and nothing more; women, their rights and nothing less.

Susan B Anthony (1820-1906) US writer and women's rights campaigner.

Catch 22

What sane person could live in this world and not be crazy?

Ursula K Le Guin (1929-   ) US writer.

Grand passion

We are minor in everything but our passions.

Elizabeth Bowen (1899-1973) Irish writer.

Idealism

I am in the world to change the world.

Käthe Kollwitz (1867-1945) German artist.

Women

The 21st century must belong to women. We survivors of the most violent century in history wish for new utopias. The millennium which begins with this 21st century grants us at least the right to imagine good and better times. May this new era be more humane and plural where gender will no longer be a category for classifying people but culturally enriching criterion, with greater diversity, for all societies. Let us celebrate then, this century, as our century.

Irma Arriagada Chilean sociologist.

Real friends

When someone tells you the truth, lets you think for yourself, experience your own emotions, s/he is treating you as a true equal. As a friend.

Whitney Otto, contemporary US writer.

All in the mind

When women are depressed, they eat or go shopping. Men invade another country. It's a whole different way of thinking.

Elayne Boolser (1952-   ) US comedian.

Who's who?

For most of history, Anonymous was a woman.

Virginia Woolf (1882-1941) British writer.

If only

The bitterest tears shed over graves are for words left unsaid and deeds left undone.

Harriet Beecher Stowe (1811-1896) US writer.

Love is all

There is only one happiness in life, to love and be loved.

George Sand (1804-1876) French writer.

War machine

When I was growing up, it was 'Communists'. Now it's 'Terrorists'. So you always have to have somebody to fight and be afraid of, so the war machine can build more bombs, guns, and bullets and everything.

Cindy Sheehan (b 1957) US anti-war activist.

Waywardness

I used to be Snow White but I drifted.

Mae West (1892-1980) US actress.

About New Internationalist Publications

New Internationalist is a publications co-operative based in Oxford, UK, with editorial and sales offices in New Zealand/Aotearoa, Australia and Canada.

It publishes the **New Internationalist** magazine on global issues, which has 65,000 subscribers worldwide. The NI also produces the One World Calendar, Almanac and Greetings Cards, as well as publications such as *Yasuní Green Gold* and food books including *Street Food* and *Vegetarian Quick & Easy* - cooking from around the world.

For more information write to:

Aotearoa/New Zealand PO Box 35038, Christchurch. newint@chch. planet.org.nz

Australia and PNG 28 Austin Street, Adelaide 5000, South Australia. helenp@newint.com.au

Canada and US 401 Richmond Street West, Studio 393, Toronto, Ontario M5V 3A8. nican@web.ca

United Kingdom 55 Rectory Road, Oxford OX4 1BW. ni@newint.org

Visit the **NI** website at **www.newint.org**

THE LITTLE BOOK OF BIG IDEAS

Thoughts on the important things in life.

Collected by Vanessa Baird

When an idea is wanting, a word can always be found to take its place,' said Goethe. This little book is the exact opposite. It's rich in ideas, economic in words. Put the world's greatest thinkers in our pocket. This little book captures the essence of some of the biggest ideas – from Gaia to Chaos theory, from Communism to Eco-Feminism, from the 'end of History' to racial equality. It provides food for both cogitation and inspiration – ideal for the busy person with more brain than time. In their own words, enjoy the ideas and ideals of thinkers and activists such as:

James Lovelock, Vandana Shiva, EF Schumacher, Eduardo Galeano, Angela Davis, Francis Fukuyama, James Gleick, Nelson Mandela, Audre Lorde, Socrates, Kenneth Kaunda, Karl Marx, Bertrand Russell, Mahatma Gandhi, Albert Einstein, Germaine Greer, Mark Twain, the Dalai Lama, Barack Obama.
This small book will easily fit into a handbag or pocket. It can be read right through or dipped into and used on a 'thought for the day' basis, on the bus, on the train, anywhere.

ISBN 978-1-906523-21-3

THE LITTLE BOOK OF AFRICAN WISDOM
Proverbs from Africa and the Caribbean

Collected by PATRICK IBEKWE

'Do not blame God for having created the tiger, but thank him for not having given it wings.' Amharic/Ethiopia

'He who loves, loves you with your dirt.' Uganda

'Hate people, but don't give them baskets to fetch water in.' Trinidad

No great deeds, works of art or books of history reveal so muc about a culture as the folklore and collective wisdom of i sayings. All over Africa, and throughout the Caribbean and th United States there is a rich and robust oral black tradition whic has been lovingly collected by **PATRICK IBEKWE** in this boo The quotations are attractively presented on the page with range of designs, motifs, sculptures and carvings which pick u on the sentiments expressed. Easy to browse through, this boo is an inspiration for lessons, speeches or articles and for all love of African culture.

from New Internationalist Publications **www.newint.org**

ISBN 978-1-906523-20-6